ANTONIO VIVALDI

LA PRIMAVERA
SPRING
DER FRÜHLING
LE PRINTEMPS

Concerto for Violin, Strings and Basso continuo
E major/E-Dur/Mi majeur
Op. 8/1
(RV 269)
Edited by/Herausgegeben von/Édition
Simon Launchbury

CONTENTS/INHALT/CONTENU

Preface III
Vorwort IV
Préface V
Sonnet/Sonett/Sonnet VI
Textual Notes/Einzelanmerkungen/Appareil critique VIII

Concerto No. 1 'La Primavera'
  I. Allegro 1
  II. Largo e pianissimo sempre 11
  III. Allegro. Danza Pastorale. 15

Performing material based on this edition is available from the publisher/
Der hier veröffentlichte Notentext ist auch als Aufführungsmaterial beim Verlag erhältlich/
Le matériel d'exécution réalisé à partir de cette édition est disponible chez l'éditeur

PREFACE

The *Four Seasons* are the first four of twelve concertos published as the *opera ottava* of Vivaldi by Le Cene of Amsterdam c.1725 with the title: 'Il Cimento dell' Armonia e dell' Invenzione' ('The Contest of Harmony and Invention'). Vivaldi added titles to several of his works, as was fashionable at the time, but the *Four Seasons* are unique in that they are prefaced by descriptive sonnets, assumed to be by the composer himself, which, as he writes in the dedicatory epistle, '[. . .] explain the music more easily'. The sections of the sonnets were initialled and the phrases inserted in the instrumental parts at the appropriate place. As well as the sonnets themselves, Vivaldi also added narrative captions to certain passages to highlight the descriptive nature of the music. This text matter is set out in a conflicting and generally haphazard manner in the source and a certain amount of tacit editorial adjustment has been made in the present edition particularly concerning the consistency of spelling and capitalization.

As there is no extant autograph the present edition is based on a copy of the early edition by Le Cene, now in the British Library, London (detailed in the Textual Notes below). This source contains many phrasing and dynamic markings, and any editorial additions are for the sake of conformity between identical sections and unanimity between the parts; these are indicated within square brackets or in the case of slurs and ties as broken ligatures. The notational distinction of the two forms of staccato marking found in the source (i.e., the stroke and the dot) has been retained in this edition. Where a tempo indication appears with a dynamic mark in the source, e.g., *p e larghetto*, the tempo mark is placed above the system and the dynamic marking below in this edition.

The term *Organo* in the instrumental bass section is taken to mean an appropriate keyboard instrument, most certainly a harpsichord in the present context. The indication *Tasto solo* (without harmonization) is only occasionally terminated with a *Tutti* marking in the source; other necessary *Tutti* markings have been supplied editorially.

The Italian commentary – based on the prefatory sonnets – contains some minor inconsistencies of spelling, capitalization, punctuation, etc., in the sources. These texts have not been modernized in this edition neither have they been detailed in the Textual Notes.

Simon Launchbury

VORWORT

Die *Vier Jahreszeiten* sind die ersten der zwölf als op. 8 (*opera ottava*) erschienenen Konzerte von Vivaldi, die um 1725 von Le Cene in Amsterdam unter dem Titel *Il Cimento dell'Armonia e dell' Invenzione* („Der Wettstreit zwischen Harmonie und Einfall") herausgegeben wurden. Der damaligen Mode entsprechend hat Vivaldi mehreren seiner Werke einen Titel gegeben; die *Vier Jahreszeiten* sind jedoch insofern einzigartig, als ihnen Sonette vorangestellt sind, die vermutlich vom Komponisten selbst stammen und über die er in seinem Widmungsschreiben äußert, sie „sollten die Musik verständlicher machen". Den einzelnen Abschnitten der Sonette sind Großbuchstaben vorangestellt, und die Worte der Sonette stehen in den Stimmen an entsprechender Stelle. Vivaldi hat neben den Sonetten zudem beschreibende Überschriften für bestimmte Passagen eingefügt, um den deskriptiven Charakter der Musik herauszustellen. Dieser Aspekt des Textanteils in den *Vier Jahreszeiten* stellt sich in der Quelle (also der Erstausgabe) auf widersprüchliche und durchweg zufällige Art und Weise dar; so hat der Herausgeber dieser Ausgabe prinzipiell bestimmte Berichtigungen besonders im Hinblick auf Übereinstimmung von Wortlaut und den erwähnten Großbuchstaben stillschweigend vorgenommen.

Das Autograph ist nicht erhalten; deshalb beruht diese Ausgabe auf einem Exemplar der Erstausgabe von Le Cene. Es ist heute im Besitz der British Library, London, und wird in den Einzelanmerkungen näher beschrieben. Diese Quelle enthält viele Eintragungen für Phrasierungen und Dynamik. Herausgeberzusätze stellen die Übereinstimmung identischer Stellen und der Stimmen untereinander sicher. Man erkennt sie an eckigen Klammern oder gestrichelten Phrasierungs- oder Legato-

bögen. Keil und Punkt als *staccato*-Vorschrift sind in dieser Ausgabe gemäß der Quelle beibehalten. Bei Tempo-Angaben mit dem Zusatz einer dynamischen Vorschrift, beispielsweise *p e larghetto*, steht in dieser Ausgabe die Vorschrift für das Tempo über dem System, für die Dynamik darunter.

Mit *Organo* in der Baßgruppe ist ein geeignetes Tasteninstrument gemeint, hier mit großer Wahrscheinlichkeit ein Cembalo. Am Ende einer *Tasto solo*-Passage (also ohne Harmonisierung) steht in der Quelle nicht immer *Tutti*. Diese und weitere *Tutti*-Vorschriften hat der Herausgeber hinzugesetzt.

Der italienische Kommentar auf der Grundlage der vorangestellten Sonette enthält in den Quellen einige unbedeutende Widersprüche in Schreibweise, Großschreibung, Zeichensetzung usw. In dieser Ausgabe wurden weder diese Texte modernisiert noch in den Einzelanmerkungen näher erläutert.

Simon Launchbury
Übersetzung Norbert Henning

PRÉFACE

Les *Quatre saisons* sont les quatre premiers de douze concertos publiés comme *opera ottava* de Vivaldi par Le Cene, à Amsterdam, vers 1725, sous le titre de «Il Cimento dell'Armonia e dell'Invenzione» («Le combat de l'Harmonie et de l'Invention»). Selon l'usage en faveur à son époque, Vivaldi ajouta des titres à plusieurs de ses œuvres mais les *Quatres saisons* représentent un cas exceptionnel à cet égard car elles sont précédées de sonnets descriptifs, sans doute écrits par le compositeur lui-même, qui, ainsi qu'il le précise dans sa dédicace, «[. . .] expliquent plus facilement la musique.» Aux différentes sections des sonnets furent attribuées des lettres et les vers furent insérés dans la partition aux endroits correspondants. En plus des sonnets, Vivaldi illustra quelques passages de légendes narratives qui soulignent la nature descriptive de ces concertos. Ces textes sont généralement placés de façon indécise et fortuite dans la source. Un certain nombre de corrections tacites ont donc été effectuées dans cette édition, notamment en ce qui concerne la cohérence de l'orthographe et des majuscules.

Comme il n'existe aucun manuscrit autographe des œuvres, notre édition s'appuie sur un exemplaire de la première édition de Le Cene conservé à la British Library de Londres (et analysé dans l'appareil critique ci-dessous). Cette source comporte de nombreuses indications de phrasé et de nuances dynamiques; les précisions éditoriales complémentaires ont pour objectif de rétablir la conformité entre sections identiques et la similarité des parties. Celles-ci sont placées entre crochets ou, dans le cas des liaisons et liaisons de phrasés, en pointillé. Les deux formes distinctes de notation du *staccato* figurant dans la source (tiret et point) ont été maintenues. Lorsque dans la source apparaît une indication de tempo accompagnée d'une nuance dynamique, par exemple *p e larghetto*, l'indication de tempo est placée au-dessus du système et l'indication dynamique en dessous.

Le terme *Organo* à la basse instrumentale désigne tout instrument à clavier approprié, et sûrement le clavecin dans ce contexte. La mention *Tasto solo* (sans harmonisation) n'est que rarement suivie de la notation de reprise du *Tutti* dans la source. Certaines indications de *Tutti* supplémentaires ont été rétablies à l'édition.

Le commentaire en italien – reposant sur les sonnets d'introduction – présente certaines incohérences mineures dans les sources quant à l'orthographe, les majuscules, la ponctuation, etc. Ces textes n'ont pas été modernisés pour cette édition, ni ne font l'objet d'une analyse dans l'appareil critique.

Simon Launchbury
Traduction Agnès Ausseur

Sonetto Dimostrativo
Sopra il Concerto Intitolato La
PRIMAVERA

DEL SIG.re D. ANTONIO VIVALDI

A Giunt' é la Primavera e festosetti
B   La Salutan gl'Augei con lieto canto,
C   Ei fonti allo Spirar de' Zeffiretti
         Con dolce mormorio Scorrono intanto:

D Vengon' coprendo l'aer di nero amanto
         E Lampi, e tuoni ad annuntiarla eletti
E   Indi tacendo questi, gl'Augelletti;
         Tornan' di nuovo allor canoro incanto:

F E quindi Sul fiorito ameno prato
         Al caro mormorio di fronde e piante
         Dorme'l Caprar col fido can'à lato.

G Di pastoral Zampogna al Suon festante
         Danzan Ninfe e Pastor nel tetto amato
         Di primavera all'apparir brillante.

Sonnet/Sonett/Sonnet

SPRING

A   Spring has arrived, and
B   the birds cheerfully greet her with joyful song,
C   while the streams, at the Zephyrs' gentle blowing,
     flow with sweet murmuring.

D   The sky becomes cloaked in amarantine black
     by the noble heralds of thunder and lightning.
E   Then silencing them, the little birds
     return to their enchanting song.

F   And so, on the pleasant flowery meadow
     to the gentle murmur of leaves and plants,
     the goatherd sleeps with his faithful dog at his side.

G   To the festive sound of country bagpipes,
     nymphs and shepherds dance beneath the beloved vault
     at the shining appearance of spring.

Translation Peter Owens

FRÜHLING

A   Der Frühling ist gekommen, und
B   freudig begrüßen ihn die Vögel mit heiterem Gesang,
C   und die Ströme fließen mit süßem Murmeln zu den leise
     wehenden Zephirwinden dahin.

D   Von Donner und Blitz, den Vorboten des Gewitters, wird
     der Himmel in ein dunkelrot-schwarzes Gewand gehüllt.
E   Zunächst verstummt, trillern die Vögelein dann wieder
     ihre bezaubernden Lieder.

F   Und auf den lieblichen Blumenwiesen,
     beim zarten Rauschen von Blättern und Pflanzen,
     schlummern Seite an Seite der Hirte und sein treuer Hund.

G   Zu den festlichen Klängen der Dudelsackpfeifer
     tanzen Nymphen und Hirten unter dem teuren Himmelszelt.
     Strahlend ist der Frühling erschienen.

Übersetzung Esther Dubielzig

LE PRINTEMPS

A   Le Printemps est arrivé et dans la liesse
B   les oiseaux l'accueillent de leurs chants joyeux,
C   tandis que les fontaines sous les doux souffles des Zéphyrs
     murmurent délicatement.

D   Le ciel s'assombrit de noir amarante
     annonçant le tonnerre et les éclairs.
E   Puis, les faisant taire, les petits oiseaux
     reprennent leurs chansons charmeuses.

F   Et, ainsi, dans la jolie prairie fleurie,
     au doux bruissement des feuilles et des fleurs,
     le chevrier est assoupi, son chien fidèle à côté de lui.

G   Au son allègre des cornemuses villageoises
     dansent les nymphes et les bergers sous la voûte céleste
     à l'éclatante apparition du printemps.

Traduction Agnès Ausseur

1E = First edition, undated c. 1725, in sets of parts, title-page:
IL CIMENTO DELL' ARMONIA/E DELL' IN-
VENTIONE/CONCERTI/a 4 e 5/[. . .]/DA
D. ANTONIO VIVALDI/[. . .]/OPERA OTTAVA/
Libro Primo/A AMSTERDAM/spesà di MICHELE
CARLO LE CENE/Librario/No. 520
Set consulted: British Library, London,
GB-Lbm g.33.c.

n(n) = note(s)
b(b) = bar(s)

Concerto No. 1

Mov. I

bar   46   Vla. 1st beat in 1E reads: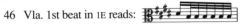

Mov. II

10   Vla. nn1, 2 b b in 1E

Mov. III

31   Vl. I nn5–6 slurred in 1E

Simon Launchbury

CONCERTO No. 1 LA PRIMAVERA

Antonio Vivaldi
(1678–1741)
Op. 8/1
RV 269

I. Allegro
A Giunt'è la Primavera

Edited by Simon Launchbury
© 1982 Ernst Eulenburg Ltd
Revised edition © 1996 Ernst Eulenburg Ltd
and Ernst Eulenburg & Co GmbH

No. 1220   EE 7036

2

B IL CANTO DE GL'UCELLI

IL CANTO DE

IL CANTO DE GL'UCELLI

GL'AUGELLI

EE 7036

e festosetti la salutan gl'augei con lieto canto,

SCORRONO I FONTI
C e i fonti allo spirar de'zeffiretti

4

con dolce mormorio scorrono intanto:

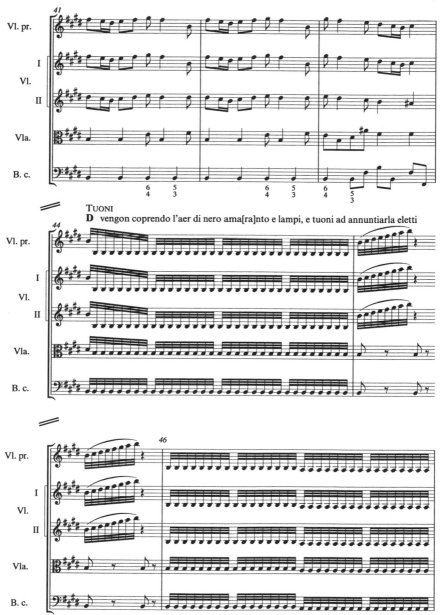

Tuoni

D vengon coprendo l'aer di nero ama[ra]nto e lampi, e tuoni ad annuntiarla eletti

6

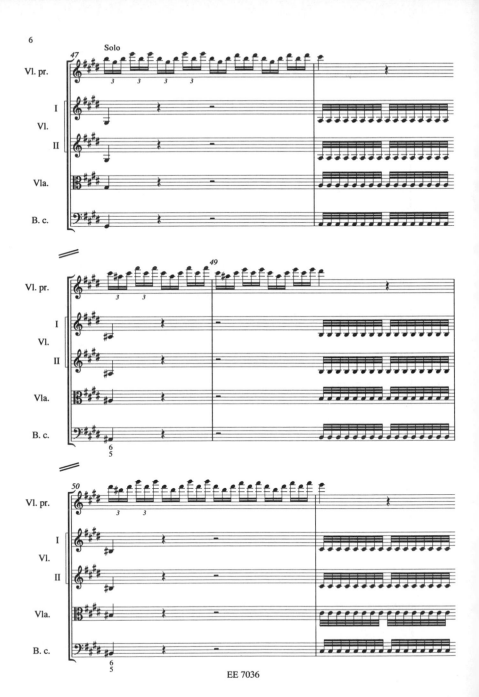

EE 7036

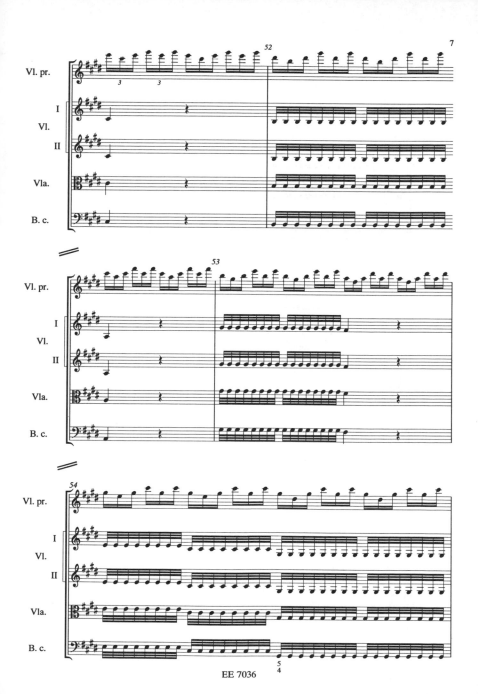

CANTO D'UCELLI
E indi tacendo questi, gl'augeletti; tornan di nuovo al lor

canoro incanto:

CANTO D'UCELLI
Solo

CANTO D'UCELLI
Solo

9

EE 7036

II. Largo e pianissimo sempre

F E quindi sul fiorito ameno prato al caro mormorio di fronde e piante

dorme'l caprar col fido can à lato.

12

14

15

III. Allegro
DANZA PASTORALE

G Di pastoral zampogna al suon festante danzan ninfe e pastor nel tetto

amato di primavera all'apparir brillante.

EE 7036

16

EE 7036

20

22